M000309317

ULTIMATE TEDDY

B·E·A·R

THE LITTLE BOOK OF

BEAR CARE

PAULINE COCKRILL

INTRODUCTION BY JUDY SPARROW

DORLING KINDERSLEY
London • New York • Stuttgart

A DORLING KINDERSLEY BOOK

PROJECT EDITOR Gillian Roberts
ART EDITOR Vicki James
MANAGING EDITOR Mary-Clare Jerram
MANAGING ART EDITOR Gill Della Casa
PRODUCTION MANAGER Eunice Paterson
PHOTOGRAPHY Matthew Ward

FIRST PUBLISHED IN GREAT BRITAIN IN 1992
BY DORLING KINDERSLEY LIMITED,
9 HENRIETTA STREET, LONDON WC2E 8PS

A CIP catalogue record for this book is available from
the British Library

ISBN 0-7513-0003-9

Computer page make-up by The Cooling Brown Partnership, Great Britain

Text film output by The Right Type, Great Britain

Reproduced by Colourscan, Singapore

Printed in Hong Kong

❧ CONTENTS ❧

❧ INTRODUCTION ❧
by Judy Sparrow

For those who inherit or buy a valuable antique bear, or
perhaps have just discovered their long-lost childhood toy in
the attic, one of the most important considerations is his
condition and future care. The love that is given to all bears by
their original owners means a hard life for Teddy. Many are
slept on, squashed, and cried over – even torn apart by jealous
brothers, or attacked by dogs. The box in the dusty attic where
Teddy has spent many years waiting
to see again the light of day may also
be home to insects, and the back
of the garage is probably damp.

---- ❧❧ ----

Almost any bear can be restored to
a sound and strong condition, but a
badly worn teddy does need expert
attention. The straightforward
repairs in this book are easy

A COLLECTOR'S BEAR
*Protect a valuable antique
bear with clothing, like this
sumptuous blue velvet
jacket and
breeches.*

enough for anybody who can sew a seam. The basic rules are: always use very strong thread; start and finish seams thoroughly; examine seams for broken stitches and resew immediately; never cut off dangling ends of paws or feet, or loose legs, arms, or ears; never use glue on the body of a fabric bear.

PATIENT BEAR
A 1950s bear waits for his operation.

Although collectable and antique bears should be restored to as near the original condition as possible, many children's toys have immense sentimental value: the pads are scraps of mummy's old skirt, or the eyes are buttons from grandma's sewing box. Changing everything on a family bear may not be necessary. However, loose limbs, and the consequent strain on a threadbare stomach from the joints, or the rusty wire of a broken squeaker, may be more dangerous to Teddy's long-term health.

Bears benefit from the right clothes – a knitted suit will protect and enhance a threadbare teddy. In the same way, correct period clothing makes it safer to handle an antique bear. Even the bear sitting at the end of a child's bed is more likely to survive for the next generation if he is clothed and cared for from the first day he is welcomed into the family.

A FAMILY BEAR
This 1950s Chad Valley bear is basically in good condition. A wash and brush-up, and a ribbon bow, are all that is needed to restore his appearance.

❧ EYES ❧

Repairing Traditional Bears

Trouser buttons are an unusual replacement for the original glass eyes.

Original mohair plush fabric, now almost worn away in places.

Alpha Toys trademark label, sewn on foot pad.

Replacement felt foot and paw pads.

1930s FARNELL BEAR

he earliest teddies had black or – occasionally – brown boot-button eyes. Blown glass eyes generally replaced these in the 1920s as buttoned boots (and their buttons) left the fashion scene. Modern replicas of both types are available but should be used only on bears that are not intended for use as children's toys.

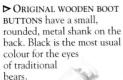

▷ ORIGINAL WOODEN BOOT BUTTONS have a small, rounded, metal shank on the back. Black is the most usual colour for the eyes of traditional bears.

▷ PLASTIC BUTTONS can replace boot buttons.

▷ POLYESTER THREAD secures the eyes through the shank.

△ CLEAR GLUE dabbed in eye socket gives a secure fixing.

◁ CLEAR GLASS EYES were often backed with brown enamel.

△ ARTISTS' ACRYLIC PAINT can be useful for colouring clear glass eyes.

▷ WIRED GLASS EYES are joined in pairs. Snip apart to make two short wire stems. Twist the wire with pliers to form a shank.

▽ MERCERIZED COTTON makes safe embroidered eyes for a child's bear.

◁ SHANKED EYES are attached by bringing strong thread through the head, into the eye socket, and through the shank. Return thread to back of head and secure with several stitches.

·❧· EYES ·❧·
Repairing Modern Bears

A sticking plaster used as a first-aid remedy for a lost eye may damage the fabric.

Yellow and black plastic safety eye is locked securely in position with a toothed washer.

This modern bear is made of good-quality, synthetic plush.

CONTEMPORARY PLUSH BEAR

By the 1950s, moulded glass and plastic eyes had become the most widely used varieties. The wire shank evolved into an integral plastic shank with a separate washer. This created the safety eye that is now required for all children's toys. Replica boot buttons and glass eyes are still commonly used for collectors' bears, to achieve a traditional appearance.

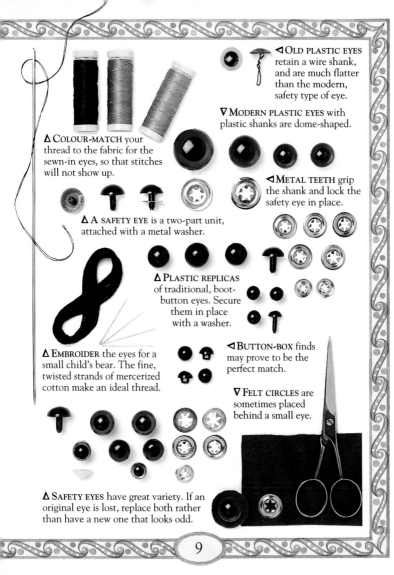

△ **COLOUR-MATCH** your thread to the fabric for the sewn-in eyes, so that stitches will not show up.

◁ **OLD PLASTIC EYES** retain a wire shank, and are much flatter than the modern, safety type of eye.

▽ **MODERN PLASTIC EYES** with plastic shanks are dome-shaped.

△ **A SAFETY EYE** is a two-part unit, attached with a metal washer.

◁ **METAL TEETH** grip the shank and lock the safety eye in place.

△ **PLASTIC REPLICAS** of traditional, boot-button eyes. Secure them in place with a washer.

△ **EMBROIDER** the eyes for a small child's bear. The fine, twisted strands of mercerized cotton make an ideal thread.

◁ **BUTTON-BOX** finds may prove to be the perfect match.

▽ **FELT CIRCLES** are sometimes placed behind a small eye.

△ **SAFETY EYES** have great variety. If an original eye is lost, replace both rather than have a new one that looks odd.

❧ NOSE & MOUTH ❧
Repairing Traditional and Modern Bears

A leather patch replaces nose and the surrounding worn fabric.

The missing mouth gives an endearing, doleful expression.

The original black leather paw pads match those on the feet.

Typical 1940s bear made of real sheepskin dyed golden brown.

1940S SHEEPSKIN BEAR

A hand-stitched nose and mouth are classic features of both traditional and modern bears. While the nose is sometimes made of moulded rubber or plastic, or even painted tin, the mouth is invariably stitched in the traditional, inverted Y-shape so often associated with bears: a central, vertical stitch with a single or double horizontal stitch.

▷ TWISTED STRANDS of thick embroidery silk or mercerized cotton are best for stitching nose and mouth details. Wool could be used for a family bear.

△ STITCHED NOSES AND MOUTHS are commonly black or brown. The vertical stitch catches a horizontal stitch to form the typical, inverted Y-shaped mouth.

 △ NEEDLES with large eyes are best.

△ TIN NOSES are more suitable for old bears. They are sewn on to the muzzle through holes at the sides of the nostrils.

△ STRONG THREAD must be used to attach sewn-on noses, but do not use such noses on a child's toy.

△ MOULDED, PLASTIC NOSES are attached with a metal washer in the same way as safety eyes.

◁ THIN, FINE LEATHER or stretchy cotton fabric are less usual, but possible, choices for the nose of a family bear.

❧·BODY FABRICS·❧

Repairing Traditional Bears

1910 Steiff bear made of black mohair plush.

Fabric often tears near joints.

Torn fabric weakens the whole arm.

Replacement beige suede leather foot pads.

1910 STEIFF BEAR

The early teddy bear manufacturers soon abandoned the expensive, real fur that had always been used for other toy animals, in favour of a newly invented and cheaper material called mohair plush. Woven from a combination of long, silky Angora-goat hair and cotton or wool, this luxurious fabric is regarded as the hallmark of a quality bear.

▷ **WOVEN MOHAIR PLUSH** comes in a wide range of traditional colours. Using any other material to patch an old mohair bear will devalue the bear, but a new piece must have the same length of pile and weave as the original fabric.

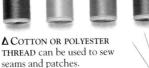

△ **COTTON OR POLYESTER THREAD** can be used to sew seams and patches.

△ **MOHAIR PLUSH** straight from the loom has long and shaggy separate strands. Clipping and brushing create a short, dense pile.

△ **DISTRESSED MOHAIR** – a 1980s' invention – is treated to look like the fabric of very old bears.

△ **MULTI-PURPOSE DYES** can darken a patching piece that has the right weave and pile, but is the wrong shade. Mix colours to get a match.

△ **THE REVERSE SIDE OF WOVEN MOHAIR** can be used to patch a bald bear. The weave should match that of the bear's original fabric to achieve the most authentic look.

△ **OLD PIECES OF FABRIC** are useful for patching a bear whose mohair has lost some of its pile.

△ **A NATURAL-FIBRE BRISTLE BRUSH** will fluff up the pile of a much-cuddled bear.

·❧· BODY FABRICS ·❧·
Repairing Modern Bears

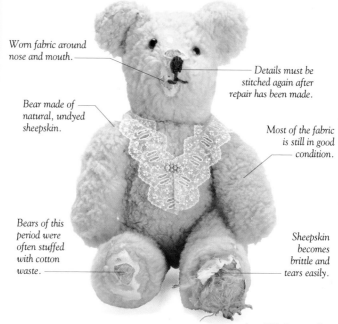

Worn fabric around nose and mouth.

Details must be stitched again after repair has been made.

Bear made of natural, undyed sheepskin.

Most of the fabric is still in good condition.

Bears of this period were often stuffed with cotton waste.

Sheepskin becomes brittle and tears easily.

LATE 1940s SHEEPSKIN BEAR

The 1940s saw the beginning of an increased popularity in materials made from synthetic fibres. Acrylic, nylon, and artificial silk plush – the most widely used fabrics – are produced on a knitted or woven backing. They make surface-washable bears that are especially suitable for children. Real mohair plush is still favoured for collectors' bears.

▷ WOVEN SHORT-PILE and DISTRESSED MOHAIR PLUSH are expensive fabrics. A modern bear's fur is probably not worn, but torn, so you may need only a small piece, such as an offcut, for patching.

▽ COTTON PLUSH is a natural fabric with a woven backing. It is a good deal cheaper than real mohair.

◁ REAL SHEEPSKIN can be difficult to work with.
▽ SYNTHETIC SHEEPSKIN makes a good alternative.

◁ THREADS for hand-stitching are stronger if used double.

△ REPAIRING SHEEPSKIN is not easy as the skin dries out with age, and often becomes too brittle to sew. A piece of supple kid leather makes an excellent repair – an old glove could provide a big enough patch. Cut a piece that is slightly larger than the damaged area and glue it to the inside with a rubber-based adhesive.

▷ SYNTHETIC FABRICS come in an enormous range of colours and finishes. A patch must match the length of pile as well as the colour of material used originally. You can clip shaggy, long-haired types to get the right length.

❊·FOOT & PAW PADS·❊

Repairing Traditional Bears

1950s bear made of golden mohair plush.

Fabric and stuffing may need total replacement.

Worn paw pad shows old cotton waste stuffing.

Original, threadbare Rexine foot pad.

Seams are often the first area to come apart.

1950s GOLDEN MOHAIR PLUSH BEAR

Felt was the most usual material for the foot and paw pads of traditional bears, and is still a good choice for patching and replacing those worn beyond repair. Rexine, a specially treated muslin that is no longer available, was used from the 1930s to about 1960. Tightly woven cotton fabric, painted with artists' quick-drying acrylic colour, makes an authentic-looking substitute.

▷ **COTTON THREAD** is best for machined seams.

◁ **HAT FELT** is used to replace dense felt pads.

▽ **CARDBOARD** reinforces the foot pads of standing bears.

▷ **NEEDLES** for hand-stitching must be sharp.

△ **POLYESTER** makes a strong thread.

△ **FLANNELETTE** was used on bears made in the 1930s.

▽ **FAKE REXINE** has a closely woven cotton base material.

△ **FELT PATCHES** must match the original fabric. Ladder-stitch neatly in place (see p.27), using polyester thread.

▽ **ACRYLIC PAINT** is applied to the fabric with a soft brush.

△ **EMBROIDERED CLAWS** in mercerized cotton add a final touch of detailing.

❧· FOOT & PAW PADS ·❧
Repairing Modern Bears

Golden mohair plush fabric is mostly in reasonable condition.

Plastic, safe eyes locked into place with a washer.

Pedigree Soft Toys bear, made in the Belfast factory around 1955.

Velveteen foot and paw pads have lost much of the surface pile, but seams are still intact.

1950S MOHAIR BEAR

ince the 1950s, a whole array of materials has joined the felt that was once used almost exclusively for bear pads. Modern-day manufacturers now have a choice between natural fabrics, such as woven cottons, velveteen, coloured felts, leather, and suede, and synthetic nylon plush, suedette, and leatherette.

▷ **POLYESTER** and **COTTON THREAD** are equally suitable for hand-sewing patches.

▽ **CARDBOARD** or iron-on interlining can strengthen thinner fabrics.

△ **FELT** is ideal for patching and replacing pads as the edges do not fray. Thick types are hard-wearing.

◁ **LEATHERETTE** has some give, making it easier to work with than real leather.

◁ **KNITTED** fabric stretches, and will fit neatly over worn pads.

▷ **SYNTHETIC VELVET** has a close texture, almost no pile, and very little stretch.

▷ **SUEDETTE**, a synthetic material, looks quite different from suede.

▷ **COTTON VELVETEEN** has a close-woven backing and a short, thick pile.

△ **SUEDE** is expensive, but a patching piece can be cut from a new pair of cheap slippers.

◁ **WOVEN MOHAIR PLUSH** is sometimes reversed for pads.

◁ **CLIPPED NYLON PLUSH** is commonly used for pads.

▷ **THREAD** for the claws must match colour of nose and mouth.

❧·JOINTS·❧
Repairing Traditional and Modern Bears

1950s English
bear made of
mohair plush,
coloured golden
when new.

New,
boot-button
eyes.

Badly worn arm
joint needs to be
replaced.

Original flannelette
paw pads.

Original
flannelette foot pads.

1950s Mohair Bear

ost traditional bears – and traditional-style modern
ones – have a movable head and limbs. Their joints
work on the enduring principle of two discs rotating
around a pin; it is only the disc and pin materials, and the fixing
method, that have changed over the years. The modern,
washable teddy bears are usually unjointed.

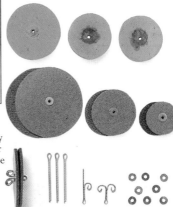

▽ **CARDBOARD** was the material from which joints were originally made. The two discs are held together by a short, metal pin inserted through a central hole, reinforced with metal washers.

△ **TO REPAIR** a traditional hardboard joint, you need two discs, two washers, and one cotter pin. Open the main body seam (see p.27). Place a disc and washer on a pin in the top of the limb, and close the seam. Push the pin into the body, slide on the disc and washer, and bend the pin ends, with pliers, close to the disc. Sew up the main seam.

△ **HARDBOARD** does not disintegrate as quickly as cardboard and so makes stronger, longer-lasting discs. Use it to cut your own discs, together with new metal washers and cotter pins.

▷ **A SPECIAL TOOL** for fixing plastic discs is available.

◁ **PLASTIC DISCS** with moulded pins and metal washers are fixed in the same way as modern safety eyes (see p.9). They form very secure joints.

△ **MODERN JOINTS** are made entirely of plastic, in a variety of sizes. Each disc has an integral, moulded pin with grooves that allow the washer to be pushed along the pin, but ensure that it cannot move once fixed in position.

❖ SOUND BOXES ❖
Repairing Traditional Bears

Early Steiff bear made of long, shaggy, black mohair plush.

Worn-out voice box can be felt inside body, but the bear produces no sound.

Main seam is at front, not back, of body.

Original wood-wool stuffing.

EARLY STEIFF BEAR

Mechanisms to give teddies a voice have been used since the early days. Punch and tilt growlers and squeakers contain a reed that produces a sound as air is forced over it. Musical boxes have worked by a clockwork movement since the 1930s; prior to this the cylinder was turned by a system of springs and levers, operated by squeezing.

▷ **EARLY TILT GROWLER** has a lead weight that opens and closes hinged bellows as the bear is tilted from back to front. The action makes a reed, attached inside a cardboard tube, vibrate.

▽ **SQUEAKERS** were used before growlers. They too contain a reed that creates the sound. The recoil of the spring inside produces the necessary rush of air as the bear is squeezed.

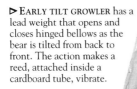

△ **THIS 1930S TILT GROWLER** has a porcelain weight with a reed set into it, and sliding oil-cloth bellows. Air and sound escape through a waxed paper membrane. The other growler shown above is contained in a cardboard container with a perforated lid that allows the sound through.

▽ **A MUSICAL BOX** contains a clockwork-driven cylinder with pins on the surface, and a metal plate divided into teeth of varying lengths. As the cylinder turns, the pins strike the teeth to produce different notes, creating a tune.

◁ **WOOD WOOL** around a new voice box allows air to be sucked in, but cannot clog the mechanism. An old box may be past repair, except by a specialist (see p.39).

23

❧ SOUND BOXES ❧

Repairing Modern Bears

1980s bear made of golden nylon plush.

Bear has been slept on, flattening the tummy fabric and squashing the squeaker.

Dark brown velveteen foot and paw pads.

1980s NYLON PLUSH BEAR

odern voice-making devices are essentially the same as those used in older bears. Growlers still contain a weight, bellows, and reed, now enclosed in a plastic case. Squeakers – invariably made of thin plastic – still contain a reed, but are now enclosed in a plastic tube. Musical boxes are wound using a pull cord or key.

▷ **GROWLER MECHANISMS** have been housed inside moulded plastic canisters since the 1940s. The whole unit may lack the aesthetic appeal of earlier models, but it does the job just as efficiently, and withstands a considerable amount of rough and tumble.

▽ **PLASTIC SQUEAKERS** come in various forms; they may be flat, concertina, or barrel-shaped with a spring. The squeak is produced by the vibration of a metal and plastic reed, protected by a hollow, plastic tube.

◁ **BELLS** in the ears were first used in 1957 by the British company, Merrythought. Although other bear manufacturers copied this idea, bells have never been as popular as squeakers and growlers.

▽ **POLYESTER** is the best stuffing to pack around a modern bear's voice box. The fine fibres in kapok (see p.29) make this an unsuitable material for the job.

▷ **PLASTIC CASES** enclose many modern musical boxes. The clockwork movement here is probably Japanese and can be activated by a nylon pull cord.

◁ **MUSICAL BOXES** work on the original principle: metal teeth of different lengths strike against pins on a revolving cylinder, sounding different notes to create a tune.

❧· SEAMS ·❧
Repairing Traditional and Modern Bears

Original, long mohair plush is very worn and dirty.

Machine-sewn front seam shows that main, hand-stitched, body seam is at back of bear.

Emergency bandage holds together a split seam.

Wood-wool stuffing.

Dirty pink velveteen pads can be surface-washed or replaced.

1930s MOHAIR BEAR

Whether old or new, a bear is made from pieces of fabric, most of which are sewn together by machine. The main body seam is the important exception: it is always stitched by hand. Bears are often flung around and carried by their limbs, so the arm and leg seams are the ones that are most likely to come adrift.

∇ **LADDER STITCH** is neater than oversewing for externally sewn seams. Fold under the raw edges. Bring up the thread from inside, cross to the other side, and take a stitch behind, along the channel, coming out just above.

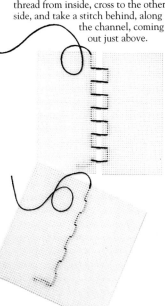

◁ **THREADS** for sewing seams by hand should be of heavier weight than all-purpose cottons. The type sold for top-stitching is ideal, or use ordinary thread doubled.

△ **POLYESTER THREAD** withstands strain rather better than cotton. Whichever you use, choose a colour that blends with the fabric.

△ **PULL UP THE THREAD** after every two or three stitches, to bring the sides of the seam together. The tiny stitches on the outside of the join will be barely visible. Finish off firmly at the end of the seam. Use this stitch for patching.

△ **THE MAIN SEAM** running the length of the bear's body is the only point of access for major body repairs, such as renewing joints (see p.21) or replacing the sound box (see pp.23 & 25). It is usually at the back, but is at the front on early Steiff bears. The last seam to be completed, it is stitched by hand.

❧· STUFFINGS ·❧
Repairing Traditional and Modern Bears

Joints rub against stuffing, causing it and the fabric to wear thin.

Stuffing is often lost first around top of arms.

British bear in need of complete overhaul.

Original wood-wool stuffing.

EARLY 1930s MOHAIR BEAR

The material with which a bear is stuffed rapidly transforms a few pieces of fabric into a cuddly friend. The early manufacturers used wood wool, and then kapok. Later, shredded plastic foam – popular from the 1950s – ensured a fully washable bear. Nowadays, polyester wadding satisfies even the most stringent modern safety standards.

▷ **WOOD WOOL** is made from long, fine wood-shavings, chopped into shorter strands. It is now quite hard to find. Old fairground toys often contain wood wool, and may yield enough for a small repair.

◁ **SILKY KAPOK** attracts neither insects nor rodents and is a good choice for a natural fibre stuffing. Do not use it for packing around a squeaker or growler; fine fibres will congest the mechanism.

▷ **SHREDDED PLASTIC FOAM** has some advantage over natural materials. Bears stuffed with it can be immersed in water for washing – but remember that burning foam emits toxic fumes.

◁ **POLYESTER WADDING** stuffs many modern bears, particularly unjointed types. It is a cheap, hygienic, safe filling for a family bear, and is ideal for packing sound boxes (see p.25).

▷ **ACRYLIC WASTE** is the modern, synthetic version of the various stuffings that once utilized the waste materials of cotton and woollen mills. It is important, when replacing a bear's stuffing, to try to use the same type as the original, so even this material has its place.

❧ WASHING ❧

Caring for Traditional and Modern Bears

New amber
and black glass
eyes.

Nose and mouth have
been restitched to
match claws.

Mohair plush is
quite dirty where
pile has been
lost.

Worn foot
pads have been
repaired before
washing
bear.

1930s CHAD VALLEY BEAR

A clean bear not only looks his best, but also has a longer life than his grubby, neglected cousin. The body fabric of most teddies can at least be surface-washed, although felt, velveteen, and cotton plush cannot. Check for insect damage (see p.37) and mend any damaged parts before starting to spruce up your bear.

▷ A BABY'S BRUSH and COMB are gentle enough to use on old and fragile fabrics.

▽ COTTON TOWELLING quickly absorbs any excess moisture. Use white cloths to avoid any colour bleeding into the bear's fabric.

△ LIQUID DETERGENT dissolves completely in cool water. Use only the foam to get rid of surface dust and static, then wipe bear with a washcloth rinsed in clean water.

▽ NATURAL SPONGES can take the place of a soft brush or cloth.

△ A BRISTLE BRUSH is ideal for removing loose dust from the pile before cleaning or washing.

◁ MACHINE-WASHING is the worst method of cleaning a jointed bear. The fabric may be revitalized but cardboard joints will disintegrate and metal washers and pins will rust. Bears that can be put safely through the rigours of laundering are usually unjointed and made from synthetics.

❧ GROOMING ❧
Caring for Traditional and Modern Bears

British bear
made of woven
nylon plush.

Ears are of a piece
with the unjointed
head.

Original maker's
label sewn on foot
pad indicates that
bear can be
washed.

Unjointed arms
and legs.

1960s WENDY BOSTON BEAR

Any cleaning process that involves getting fabric even
slightly wet must be followed by thorough drying or
the material may go mouldy and rot. Teddies, being
essentially textiles, are no exception to this rule. Laundered
bears are better dried in a mesh bag on the washing-line
than being tumble-dried in a machine.

▷ **A HAIRDRYER** with variable settings provides an even source of gentle heat. Switch it to the coolest temperature and lowest speed. Hold it at least 30cm (12in) away from your bear, and keep it moving over the whole surface of the fabric.

△ **TOWEL-DRY** a long-haired bear with a thick towel to get rid of drips. Continue the drying process with an overnight sojourn in a warm airing cupboard.

◁ **COMB** or **BRUSH** the pile once the fabric is completely dry. A soft-bristled brush and nylon comb are best for real mohair plush bears.

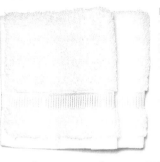

△ **SYNTHETIC FABRICS** on a knitted backing are quite robust and need not be handled as gently as woven plush. After drying, brush with a stiff, natural bristle brush to restore the pile.

MUSLIN ▷ polishes glass or button eyes.

△ **COTTON PLUSH** should not be washed, but can be reconditioned using a teasel brush.

◁ **A TEASEL BRUSH** has short, fine wire "bristles" that separate the fibres of the fabric. Brush firmly in the direction of the pile.

◁ **COTTON BUDS** are handy for getting the last drops of water out of tiny crevices.

❧ · BEAR WEAR · ❧
Accessories for Traditional and Modern Bears

New button eyes replace original black boot buttons.

Elderly bear has been sympathetically restored.

Golden mohair plush has lost most of its pile.

Blue velvet suit, trimmed with lace, protects worn fabric.

PRE-1910 STEIFF BEAR

very bear is enhanced by a bit of ornamentation. It can be as simple as a brightly coloured ribbon bow around his neck, or as grand as a designer outfit. Clothing has a practical purpose, too, as it protects the fabric from the general wear and tear that even affectionate handling will cause. It is also useful for disguising imperfections in your bear.

▷ **RIBBONS** come in an enormous variety of colours, patterns, finishes, and widths. Use them on their own, plaited together, or as trimmings for hand-sewn garments.

▷ **LACE,** slotted with ribbon, ties into a frilly collar.

△ **BELLS** are jolly, strung on pretty ribbon and tied around the neck.

△ **MINIATURE SPECTACLES** and accessories are available from toy suppliers.

△ **HAND-SEWN GARMENTS** have a personal appeal when made from scraps of your old clothes. Or buy a remnant of a really expensive fabric, such as embroidered brocade – just a small remnant will make a gorgeous jacket or waistcoat.

▷ **STRETCHY SOCKS** can cover foot pads that are past repair.

❧· STORAGE ·❧
Caring for Traditional and Modern Bears

Careful surface-washing has restored the fluffiness of the pile.

Repaired, washed, and groomed bear, ready for storage.

Lace collar and ribbon bow add a nice finishing touch.

New foot and paw pads made of felt.

1930S PINK MOHAIR PLUSH BEAR

eddies and hugs go naturally together, but handling an antique bear does not prolong his life. Instead, store him in a warm, dry place with a consistent temperature and check his condition often. The worst place for a bear is on your bed where he will be moved frequently. Keep your bear in a dust-free environment, and avoid direct sunlight.

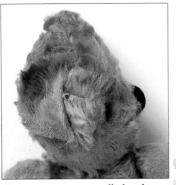

△ LARVAE CASINGS, usually found in snug places, reveal the presence of beetles or moths.

▽ PLASTIC BAGS are for brief storage only. Seal a moth-eaten bear in a plastic bag with moth balls to kill insects.

◁ MOTH BALLS act rapidly to kill moths.

◁ BROWN PAPER, tied with string, lets the bear breathe, and allows moisture to evaporate.

△ CEDAR WOOD is a natural moth repellent.

▽ WHITE TISSUE PAPER protects a fragile bear that is to be stored in a box. Use the acid-free type that does not deteriorate with age.

▽ SHOE BOXES are roomy enough for a small teddy.

❧ BEAR OWNERS ❧

Dorling Kinderseley would like to thank the following people who generously lent their injured bears for photography:

• Mrs Baker for Goldie page 31
• Gill Della Casa for Tessa pages 5 (bottom) and 37
• Vicki James for Louise pages 1 and 8
• Mary-Clare Jerram for Teddy page 27
• Mrs Lavery for Teddy page 14

• Gillian Lister for Edward page 10
• Mrs Meeke for Max page 12
• Mrs Pearce for Rupert pages 28 and 38
• Judy Sparrow for Albert pages 4, 34, and 39; Lucy page 36; Rowan pages 1 and 30; and Timmy page 20
• Mrs Spencer for David pages 3 and 16
• Mrs Tuke for Wingo pages 5 (top) and 26
• Paul & Rosemary Volpp for Sir Loved A Lot page 6 and Inky page 22
• Leah Ward for Billy page 24
• Mrs Whellams for Michael page 41
• Lynnet Wilson for Cully page 32

❧ USEFUL ADDRESSES ❧

The following addresses are given in good faith, but are not intended as a recommendation. Before sending a bear for restoration, satisfy yourself that the repairer is capable of carrying out the work to your own satisfaction. Neither the author nor the publisher can accept responsibility for the quality of any work that is carried out.

NB If sending by post (but it is safer to deliver personally) always send by Registered Delivery; check the address of the repairer first; pack the bear with all the appropriate loose parts and details of the problems.

Judy Sparrow
The Bear Museum
38 Dragon Street, Petersfield
Hampshire GU31 4JJ
☎ 0730 265108

Brian John Beacock
76 Shortwood Avenue, Staines
Middlesex TW18 4JL
☎ 0784 451631

Joan Crosbie's Hospital for Sick Teddy Bears
Three Bears Cottage
39 Wellington Road
Dartford, Kent DA1 3EH
☎ 0322 270197

Sue Pearson
13½ Prince Albert Street
The Lanes, Brighton
Sussex BN1 1HE
☎ 0273 29247

John Smith
The Dolls' Hospital
16 Dawes Road, Fulham
London SW6 7EN
☎ 071 385 2081

MAGAZINES

Hugglets Teddy Bear Magazine
Glenn Jackman
PO Box 290
Brighton BN2 1DR
☎ 0273 697974

Teddy Bear Times
Ashdown Publishing
Shelley House
104 High Street, Steyning
West Sussex BN4 3RD
☎ 0903 816111

❖· INDEX ·❖

❧ ACKNOWLEDGMENTS ❧

Dorling Kindersley would like to thank Judy Sparrow for supplying
most of the materials for photography.

We would also like to thank the following for their help:
Christabel Grimmer and Oakley Fabrics Limited for supplying materials
for photography; Andrea Fair for ferrying teddy bears to and from The Bear
Museum; Irene Lyford and Susan Thompson for editorial assistance;
Pauline Bayne and Sam Grimmer for design assistance; Peter Howlett
and Alastair Wardle for their DTP expertise.

All photographs by Matthew Ward except: Jim Coit 6, 22;
Roland Kemp 7 (step-by-step), 10, 18, 21 (step-by-step), 32.

Border illustrations by Pauline Bayne.
Illustrated letters by Gillie Newman.

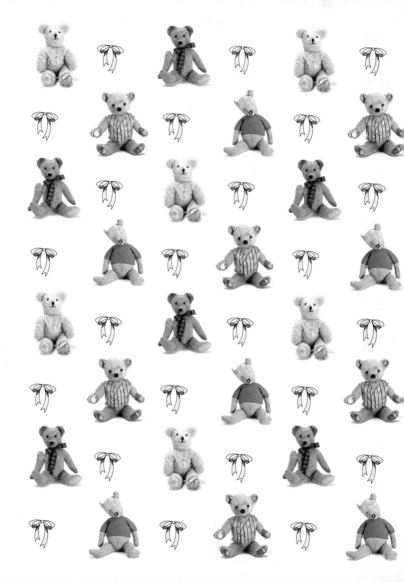